THE PRIEST AND THE PROTESTANT WOMAN

Maynooth Studies in Local History

GENERAL EDITOR Raymond Gillespie

This is one of the new pamphlets published in 1997 in the Maynooth Studies in Local History series. Like earlier titles in the series, published in 1995 and 1996, each study is derived from a thesis completed in connection with the Maynooth M.A. course in local history.

The localities studied are defined not by administrative boundaries but by the nature of the community bonds which shaped people's experiences in the past, both holding them together and driving them apart. Ranging across family, village, parish, town, and estate, the pamphlets investigate how people in these varied communities lived out their lives and responded to changes in the outside world.

These Maynooth Studies in Local History explore the richness and diversity of the Irish historical experience, and in doing so present local history as the vibrant and challenging discipline that it is.

Maynooth Studies in Local History: Number 11

The Priest
and
The Protestant Woman

Proinnsíos Ó Duigneáin

IRISH ACADEMIC PRESS

Set in 10 on 12 point Bembo by
Carrigboy Typesetting Services, Co. Cork
and published by
IRISH ACADEMIC PRESS LTD
Northumberland House
44, Northumberland Road, Ballsbridge, Dublin 4, Ireland
and in North America by
IRISH ACADEMIC PRESS LTD
c/o ISBS, 5804 NE Hassalo Street, Portland, OR 97123

A catalogue record for this title
is available from the British Library.

ISBN 0-7165-2639-5

Printed in Ireland
by ColourBooks, Dublin

Contents

Preface

For their assistance in the research of this pamphlet I wish to acknowledge the staffs of the following institutions: The National Library of Ireland; the National Archives; the Library of St Patrick's College, Maynooth; the Library of the Grand Masonic Lodge, Dublin; Trinity College Library; the National Gallery of Ireland; the Royal Irish Academy; the Dublin Diocesan Library and Roscommon, Sligo, Leitrim and Enniskillen Libraries.

I am deeply indebted to the County Leitrim librarian, Seán Ó Suilleabháin, for his unfailing courtesy and co-operation.

I am also obliged to Dr Thomas Ó Connor and Dr Raymond Gillespie of the Department of Modern History, St Patrick's College, Maynooth and to my colleagues in the MA class 1994–96 for their help, advice and friendship.

Finally, thanks to my wife Betty and my daughter Aoife for layout and typing.

Introduction

Reverend Thomas Maguire, parish priest of Drumkeerin, county Leitrim, was arraigned on a charge of seduction in the court of exchequer, Dublin in December 1827. The girl involved was Anne McGarrahan, the daughter of the village innkeeper Bartholomew McGarrahan. She was a Protestant. Fr Maguire first met Anne when he stayed for six weeks in her father's inn after his appointment to Drumkeerin in February 1825. When he acquired a house of his own he moved out of the village.

This pamphlet seeks to demonstrate how this event affected not only local sensibilities but achieved a national significance at a time of tension between two local communities, the Protestant and the Catholic. The involvement of leading lawyers and politicians such as Daniel O'Connell, Richard Sheil, Dominic Ronayne, John Henry North and others guaranteed the interest of newspaper reporters whose accounts of the priest's trial were given front-page prominence in the national and provincial press. An attempt is also made in this account to examine life in a tiny rural village at a particular time in its existence – a village which was not on the tourist trail nor considered worthy of inclusion in the nineteenth century directories.

No in-depth analyses of the Maguire/McGarrahan case have been published nor has its effect on the local community been studied. Local historians have shown a reluctance to write about a topic which has been regarded for years as a contentious issue in the diocese of Kilmore. Moreover researchers have refrained from examining an event which was considered an unsavoury one in the north-west. This seduction trial and the circumstances surrounding it are important for the glimpses provided of village life, of the parish clergy and the personalities who were influential players in the religious rivalry at national and local levels. It also affords an insight into: the male view of female sexuality, rural poverty, the vulnerability of a religious minority, migratory labour and clerical celibacy. There is no full-length biography of Rev Thomas Maguire in existence but a number of articles on aspects of his life and career have been published. Rev Raymond McGovern discusses Maguire as a preacher and politician in *Breifne* iv no. 14 (1971) pp. 277–288. Maguire's role in the Clare election of 1828 is analysed in *Breifne* i no. 1 (1959) pp. 56–59. There are some references to him in Rev Donal Kerr's article on Dr James Brown, bishop of Kilmore (1829–65) in *Breifne* vi, no. 22 (1984) pp. 109–154. Philip O'Connell gives a brief account of Maguire's career in *The Diocese of Kilmore, Its History and Antiquities*, (Dublin, 1937) pp. 536–537. In *Sliabh an*

Iarainn Slopes (1991) pp. 169–174, Fr Dan Gallogley highlights the main events in Maguire's career. Peter S. Clancy in *Innishmagrath* (1958) pp. 52–60 treats of Maguire's life in his section on the parish's Catholic clergy. Finally, there are brief notes on his life in the unpublished papers of Rev Owen Francis Traynor in the Kilmore Diocesan Archives, Bishop's House, Cullies, Cavan.

My main primary source for this study is the transcript of the trial published by N. Harding, 7 Werburgh Street in 1862. This is a copy of a transcript done by J. Mongan, barrister-at-law and published by Westlay and Tyrrell, Dublin early in 1828 – *A Report of the trial of the action in which Bartholomew M'Garahan was the plaintiff and the Reverend Thomas Maguire was the defendant ...* Dec 1827. However it is clear from the summing-up by the defence that not all questions and answers were recorded by the notetaker and in some instances the questions put to witnesses were omitted – the answers only were noted. It is also clear that there are a few small discrepancies between newspaper accounts and the published transcript. But the biggest problem presented by the trial reports is the reliability of the evidence presented. For example Anne McGarrahan's statement that the two Catholic bishops of the diocese met Maguire a few months before the trial would indicate the seriousness with which the Catholic authorities were treating the matter. However, since her allegation cannot be verified in the absence of corroborating evidence, we are left in the realm of surmise. The fact that the diocese of Kilmore actually did have a bishop and a recently appointed coadjutor, in the autumn of 1827 cannot be accepted as giving credence to her statement.

I have consulted three local papers, the *Roscommon and Leitrim Gazette*, *The Enniskillen and Erne Packet* and the *Sligo Journal* for background to the trial and for its aftermath. In the main these papers show an anti-Catholic bias but this is balanced by their quoting of the *Morning Register* and *Weekly Register*, which published reports more favourable to Fr Maguire. The *Roscommon and Leitrim Gazette* is perhaps the most reliable because it would appear that its editor, in the interests of filling up space, was willing to publish lengthy unedited accounts from both sides of the religious divide!

The State of the Country Papers in the National Archive are quite fragmentary for county Leitrim in the 1820s and they do not cover the period of the trial itself. However they are of great benefit in setting the scene and establishing the background of events in Drumkeerin village – and of course it is in a police-report that there is the first indication of the religious conflict involving Fr Maguire and Anne McGarrahan. Very valuable primary sources are the judgements delivered in February 1828 by four judges of the court of exchequer when application was made to have the verdict of the December 1827 trial set aside. These sources give additional information on the trial and also throw light on the personal biases and attitudes of the court of exchequer judges regarding the religious tensions of the time. I found the Masonic Records for the lodge in Drumkeerin useful. These records comprise registers of members and dates of acceptance plus some correspondence. There is no direct reference however to the trial in the Drumkeerin record. An examination of the material relating to other lodges in Leitrim, particularly those of Carrick-on-Shannon would probably throw further light on the personalities and the events of 1826/27.

Sources which would have been of great value in this research do not exist for the Drumkeerin area in the 1820s. There are no surviving registers of the Catholic and Protestant Churches and no Vestry Minute Books. In addition, grand jury records for the county of Leitrim before the Famine have not survived.

The opening chapter examines the national and regional contexts of the 1820s religious conflict and includes a discussion of the public debate in Dublin between Rev Thomas Maguire and Rev Richard Pope. It considers developments within county Leitrim 1826–27 in the context of the religious rivalry and tensions and a brief analysis of the village of Drumkeerin in 1827 with particular emphasis on the religious divide. The second chapter is devoted to the trial itself and especially to those sections of it which throw light on the personalities who were prominent in the village and county. The third chapter describes and analyses the effects of the trial in Dublin, in Leitrim and in Drumkeerin village. The conclusion briefly sketches the subsequent career of Rev Thomas Maguire from the aftermath of the 1827 trial up to his murder in 1847.

The Religious Conflict

The trial of Rev Thomas Maguire P.P. in December 1827 took place when the evangelical movement known as the Second Reformation was at its height. Indeed the years 1826 and 1827 witnessed intense Protestant missionary activity, especially in an area stretching from Leitrim to Louth and including North Roscommon, Fermanagh, Cavan, part of Meath and Down: the border region dividing the Protestant north from the Catholic south. This evangelical movement is taken to date from the year 1822 with the speech of William Magee, Protestant archbishop of Dublin, in which he stated that Catholics 'possessed a church without what we might properly call a religion'.[1] Opposition to his remarks came not only from members of the Catholic hierarchy such as Archbishop John McHale of Tuam and Bishop Warren Doyle of Kildare and Leighlin[2] but also from a number of parish priests including Rev Thomas Maguire of Drumkeerin. Although Magee's statement was clearly significant in heightening religious tension, the real influence of the Second Reformation movement manifested itself in the activities of the Bible Societies, two of which, the London Hibernian, founded in 1806 and the Baptist founded in 1814 were especially prominent in the aforementioned region. Local Catholic clergy were under no illusions as to the threat posed by these organisations. For example, in February 1826, the parish priest of Carrick-on-Shannon, county Leitrim declared that 'the mischiefs which the Bible Societies have done in rekindling the religious feuds of Ireland are beyond all calculation'.[3] Two other pieces of the Reformation machine were also important in this border region: the itinerant preachers supported by the local protestant clergy and certain landlords such as Lorton of Rockingham, county Roscommon, Archdale and Brooke in Fermanagh, Roden in Louth and Down and especially Farnham in Cavan. (An exception was the earl of Leitrim, who was singled out by Catholics as 'unbiased by sectarian feelings or sectarian distinctions').[4]

It was Farnham's success in winning people from Catholicism which led the Protestant bishop of Limerick, John Jebb to the opinion that 1827 was a year of exceptional significance in the spread of Protestantism.[5] In October of the same year, the *Roscommon and Leitrim Gazette* claimed that Mary Ann Bourke, niece of the Catholic bishop of Elphin diocese, had become a member of the Established Church.[6]

The Bible Societies and itinerant preachers emphasised the flaws, as they perceived them, in the Catholic religion in contrast to 'the pure doctrine of the Church of England'.[7] On the other hand, the criticism of those landlords, who were committed to the Second Reformation, also took the line of the untrustworthiness of Catholics vis a vis political power. The statement of Sir Henry Brooke at a Protestant meeting in Enniskillen, chaired by the high sheriff of Fermanagh, was typical – 'From passing events I perceive that it is ultimately necessary to exclude Roman Catholics from political power'. His sentiments were echoed by Edward Archdale who said – 'I am now surrounded by the descendants of the old Enniskilleners who sent out their armies joined by the tens of thousands of men who were once called and will be again, thank God – Orangemen, to crush the enemies of our constitution'. At the end of 1827, Roden refused to give a site for a new Roman Catholic church in Dundalk saying that he objected to the 'peculiar principles and doctrines' of Catholicism.[8] Lorton, Roden and Farnham attended Bible Society meetings in London in 1827. On 10 May, a meeting of the London Hibernian Society was chaired by Lorton[9] and on 21 May Roden and Farnham addressed the Society for Promoting the Reformation in Ireland. Captain J.C. Gordon, a prominent itinerant preacher, who was also present, enlightened the attendance on the 'idolatrous' nature of certain Catholic practices by describing a ceremony which had taken place in Tubbercurry, county Sligo: '20,000 paid adoration at a holy well, a holy tree and a holy stone, under the latter of which they crept in order to have themselves cleansed of their sins'.[10]

The principal itinerant preacher in the Leitrim, Roscommon and Cavan area in 1826–7 was Rev Richard Pope, a graduate of Trinity College. Between September and December 1826 he preached in a number of centres including Boyle (where he stayed in Lorton's house), Carrick-on-Shannon, Belturbet and Cavan town. In September, he, together with another highly acclaimed preacher, Joseph Woulff, issued a challenge to 'all the bishops, priests and doctors of the Church of Rome to meet publicly in a month hence in Dublin' to debate points of conflict in religious doctrine.[11] This challenge was accepted by Rev Thomas Maguire of Drumkeerin in November 1826 but the debate did not take place until the following April. Richard Pope was in Cavan town when one of the most important Catholic meetings in the history of the diocese of Kilmore took place in December 1826.[12] The hierarchy, alarmed by the number of conversions on the Farnham estate sent a deputation to investigate the problem. The primate himself, Dr Patrick Curtis led the deputation which also included Dr James Magauran, bishop of Ardagh, and John Mc Hale coadjutor bishop of Killala. The bishops met with twenty-eight parish priests and the vital concern of all was to find a capable successor to the previous coadjutor, Patrick Maguire (uncle of Rev Thomas Maguire of Drumkeerin) who had died eight months before. The incumbent Farrell O'Reilly was eighty-six at this time. Pope and four of his fellow evangelicals, Rev Mc Creith,

Rev Collins, Rev Spraight and Captain J.C. Gordon took up their positions outside Cavan chapel where the meeting was to convene. However the bishops decided to conduct their deliberations in the inn where they were staying, explaining their decision as follows:

> The Prelates and the Clergy of Kilmore assembled in the town of Cavan on Thursday [14th December] ... and intended to commence their religious proceedings in the chapel, but were prevented by five itinerant preachers who had previously collected a crowd at the chapel gate for the purpose of exciting Catholics to a breach of the peace ... When the first scheme adopted by the Biblicals was frustrated by the prudence of the Prelates, they received an insolent letter, signed by five of the Biblical gentry, who called for a public discussion with Dr. Curtis and other bishops ... From a becoming sense of their own dignity, the Prelates treated this impudent communication with silent contempt, and remaining at the inn proceeded with their important investigation.[13]

The professor of scripture in Maynooth College, Dr James Brown was chosen as coadjutor and succeeded Farrell O'Reilly in 1829.

On Friday, 26 January 1827 a Reformation meeting was held in Cavan, at which Lord Farnham, Rev J. Collins, Rev W. Athill, Captain J.C. Gordon and Rev Pope spoke. The Catholic bishops were castigated for not accepting the challenge and were accused of preferring 'a dishonourable safety to the risk of probable failure'. Farnham claimed that 450 Catholics had conformed in the previous four months.[14]

LEITRIM IN 1826/7

Two events, both seemingly innocuous, proved contentious in the religious conflict in county Leitrim in 1826/7. One, a dispute between a Catholic curate and a parishioner, pressured the bishop of the diocese into initiating an investigation and the second, a public dinner given in honour of the parish priest of Carrick-on-Shannon caused sectarian passions to be enflamed to an extraordinary degree. In both these episodes the influence of the three main strands of the Second Reformation: the Bible Societies, reforming landlords and itinerant preachers can be discerned. Some of the personalities engaged in evangelical activity outside the county were also involved in these conflicts. Both of these events are important in that they may have been instrumental in providing the immediate circumstances out of which emerged the Maguire/McGarrahan court case and they provide us with the names and backgrounds of certain people who featured in the trial.

The dispute between the priest and the parishioner hit the public headlines on the publication of a report of the London Hibernian meeting of 10

1. Map of Ireland showing Leitrim

January 1826 in the lecture room of the London Mechanics Institute with Joseph Butterworth M.P. in the chair. At this meeting Robert McGovern, formally a native of Leitrim village stated that the local parish priest Rev Bernard Cullen had intimidated him for reading the Bible and that he had caused him to be dismissed from his job. The chairman, Butterworth, accepted the account

saying that he had been appraised of the circumstances by Captain Duckworth.[15]
John Duckworth, who was English by birth, lived at Carrick-on-Shannon and
was a member of the grand jury; governor of the Leitrim Infirmary; chairman
of Carrick-on-Shannon Charitable Society and a member of the local lodge
of the Freemasons which 'flourished like the palm tree and grew like the
Cedar in Lebanon under the guidance of the good, wise and capable Brother
Duckworth who was practically its founder'.[16]

Bishop Magauran of Ardagh, in whose diocese this episode occurred, con-
vened a meeting in Leitrim village to investigate the allegation against Rev
Cullen. Among those present were James Coyne Esq. of Cartown House,
Carrick-on-Shannon, a spokesman for the Catholics in the area and Rev John
Mc Keon P.P., Carrick-on-Shannon, vicar general of the diocese. Captain
Duckworth and Captain J. H. Peyton, a county magistrate, were both there on
Coyne's invitation. Coyne would appear to have done this deliberately since
the newspaper report concentrated on the verbal confrontation between
Duckworth and Peyton which affords an insight into the religious conflict of
the time.

> *Duckworth*: Sir, you stated a short time back, that I have interested mo-
> tives in keeping these things alive.
>
> *Peyton*:   I did.
>
> *Duckworth*: Will you give me leave to ask you in what manner you
> suppose me interested?
>
> *Peyton*:   Certainly I conceive that you are paid for what you do and
> that it is an object with you to keep those societies up as
> big as you can.
>
> *Duckworth*: Allow me to assure you sir that you are mistaken.
>
> *Peyton*:   O then it is all from pure disinterestedness that you act.

Captain Duckworth then stood up and pledged himself that he held no
situation of profit nor did he receive any remuneration for his services
from any society in existence.[17]

Another Second Reformation personality who figured prominently in newspaper reports in 1826–7 was Captain Charles Cox, a member of the Leitrim
Bible Society and of the Carrick-on-Shannon Charitable Society. He was also
accused of having a vested interest in promoting the activities of the Bible
Society – specifically that he and Duckworth were selling the Bibles 'which
were sent down for nothing.'[18]

The Leitrim village meeting was not the end of the Robert McGovern
affair. In February 1826 McGovern issued a statement from London saying
that, for continuing to read the bible before he left home, he had been threat-
ened with a penance 'such as going barefoot to the chapel in a white sheet or
to go on a pilgrimage as is usual for disobeying the orders of the priest.' He had

been offered employment by Captain Duckworth on his farm but could not take it up on account of the distance from his home.[19] Whether McGovern told the truth or not is impossible to say but the fact that he was in London almost eight months before his case was taken up (at the instigation of Duckworth) by the Hibernian Society would seem to cast a doubt over his reliability as an informant.

At the public dinner given in his honour in Carrick-on-Shannon on 9 May 1826, Dr John Mc Keon P.P. had this to say: 'How delightful the prospect to behold the greater part of the Protestant and Catholic inhabitants of this town and of its vicinity assembled here this evening'. James Coyne Esq., Cartown House, presided at the head of the table and with an army officer Captain Masterson of the 87th Regiment at the foot.[20] Subsequent developments did not bear out McKeon's optimism. The dinner received enormous coverage in the *Roscommon and Leitrim Gazette* and was the subject of several lengthy anonymous letters written over many months. It became fused with the McGovern saga and both events were pivotal as far as the upsurge in sectarian emotion was concerned.

Towards the end of 1826 we find the first indications of Rev Thomas Maguire's public involvement in the religious quarrel. He attended a meeting of 'the Roman Catholics of county Leitrim' at Carrick-on-Shannon on 9 November, during which he issued a counter challenge to Rev Richard Pope. According to the newspaper report 'the speech of Mr Maguire was one of the most sporting kind and relates to proposed measures and plans for hunting the Biblicals with Mr Pope at their head. He regretted much that Mr Pope was not at their meeting'.[21]

Duckworth and Cox were resented by local Catholic leaders not only for their evangelising activities but also because they were considered English 'blow-ins'. James Coyne Esq. referred to them as 'newcomers who are trying to worm themselves into every piece of land that becomes vacant over the heads of poor people and sending them to desolation – there's the two captains – John Duckworth and Charles Cox – I don't care for a captain more than a mad dog – forming their Bible societies and their school societies and their charitable societies'. Coyne said that he himself 'did not make his money by following the fife and drum'. Roger Beirne, a leading Catholic in Carrick-on-Shannon referred to Duckworth as 'sleek, mild, modest Johnny Duckworth, commonly called Captain Duckworth, Bible Duckworth alias the Trawneen Planter'. Beirne accused Cox ('we don't know where the devil he's from') of ordering 'all his tenants under fear of being distrained to go and hear Mr. Pope'. Beirne went on to say that Duckworth's wife and the Carrick-on-Shannon rector's wife, Mrs Percy, had offered buttermilk and clothing to poor people if they would attend Protestant services.[22] Duckworth countered by stating that both Beirne and the Carrick-on-Shannon parish priest had once been members of the Charitable Society.[23]

In the north Leitrim area a number of conversions to the Protestant religion were reported in the local press in 1827. Most of these occurred in the parish of Killenummery which was in Bishop Magauran's diocese of Ardagh. In the case of one individual who recanted the newspaper reported that 'it is not a little remarkable that the person was one of Mr Maguire's congregation'.[24] These defections necessitated the dispatch of Rev Bernard Cullen, who had been involved in the Robert McGovern incident, to Killenummery on a fact-finding mission. While in Killenummery Cullen was challenged to take part in a discussion by Rev Michael Seymour, a well-known evangelical in the Sligo/Leitrim area. He declined the invitation.[25]

DUBLIN

Local tensions were not confined to Leitrim and soon spilled into other areas. The long-awaited debate between Rev Thomas Maguire and Rev Richard Pope took place in the lecture room of the Dublin Institute, Sackville Street, Dublin on 19–25 April, 1827.[26] A preliminary meeting, at which Maguire and Pope were present, had taken place on 11 April in the house of Mr Tims in Grafton Street. Maguire said that he 'avoided seeing or hearing anything from my own bishop, Dr O'Reilly. Since I came to Dublin, I have not received any communication from him, verbal or written'.[27] The debate which was co-chaired by Admiral Oliver for the Protestant and by Daniel O'Connell, the Catholic leader, for the Catholic side created enormous interest. 'Not only the arena was crowded but the entire of Sackville Street became blocked with population ... Fr Maguire had being previously quite unknown but the consummate ability with which he vindicated the articles of his creed at once transformed him into a highly remarkable character'.[28] Maguire benefitted from the knowledge of Richard Coyne, publisher to Maynooth College, who advised him to study a particular religious text which would facilitate his responses to points raised by Pope. Maguire did so and 'prepared himself for each discussion during a walk with Coyne in the Phoenix Park.'[29] At the conclusion of the debate both sides claimed victory. The Catholic celebrations were such that 'Mr Maguire accompanied by Mr Lawless had scarcely entered the carriage when the horses were removed and the vehicle dragged in triumph through the crowded street near Carlisle Bridge through Westmoreland Street, College Green, Dame Street, Parliament Street from whence turning down to the Quay it reached the chapel ... his residence since his arrival in town.'[30] This practice of supporters drawing the carriage of Fr. Maguire was repeated at the conclusion of the trial later in the year.

The 'Discussion', as it became known, catapulted Maguire into the public arena. Hailed as a hero, he found himself among the leading group of Catholic personalities in the city, a group which included the O'Gorman-Mahon,

Richard Coyne, John Lawless, Edward O'Reilly,[31] the Gaelic scholar and lexico-
grapher and of course Daniel O'Connell who reputedly presented him with
silver plate worth £1000 in honour of his victory.[32] According to the barrister
Richard Sheil 'Pope was overthrown and Fr Tom as the champion of ortho-
doxy, became the object of popular adoration'.[33] O'Connell claimed that
Maguire's triumph made him a detested figure in the eyes of supporters of the
Second Reformation and that had the Discussion not taken place he would
never have been accused of the seduction of Anne McGarrahan.[34] However,
a speech which Maguire made in Roscommon the following October, also
added to his notoriety in the eyes of the Reformers. He claimed that he had
been offered a gift of £1000 and a living worth £800 if he became a parson
of the Established Church. Power Le Poer Trench, Protestant archbishop of
Tuam, was named as the person who had offered the bribe. Trench instituted
a lawsuit against Maguire and the case was heard the following year.[35]

THE VILLAGE

The village of Drumkeerin, in the parish of Inishmagrath, county Leitrim was
approximately 50 years in existence when the trial took place in Dublin.[36]
The Church of Ireland, whose rector was one of the clergymen mentioned at
the trial, was built on the hill of Sheena in 1775 and it overlooked the single
street which stretched in a northerly direction towards Manorhamilton. In
1838, another church, the Methodist, would occupy a prominent position at
the opposite end of the village.[37]

Drumkeerin in the late 1820s comprised fifty-one houses and had a population of 284. Markets were held every Wednesday and fairs twelve times a
year. Petty sessions took place fortnightly and there was a penny post to Carrick
on Shannon.[38] The only inn in the village was owned by Anne McGarrahan's
father Batty. Situated midway on the main street, it was a focal point in the
village. Displaying the McGarrahan name over the door,[39] this two storey
building provided accommodation for guests and stabling for their horses.
Among the regular customers were the lawyers who came for the petty sessions.
One of the most popular drinks served in the inn was scaltheen, a beverage
which provoked much comment at the trial.[40] It was similar to punch with
the difference that the whiskey, water and sugar were boiled together. Meetings
and dances took place in McGarrahans and one could avail of a game of back-
gammon. Anne McGarrahan herself played this game.[41] A summerhouse, in
which there was an oval-shaped seat was located in the garden at the rear of
the house.[42] The McGarrahans owned at least one horse, Darby and they also
had a small farm.[43]

There were other public houses ('and as large too') in Drumkeerin. It is
not known how many there were in 1827 but twenty seven years later there

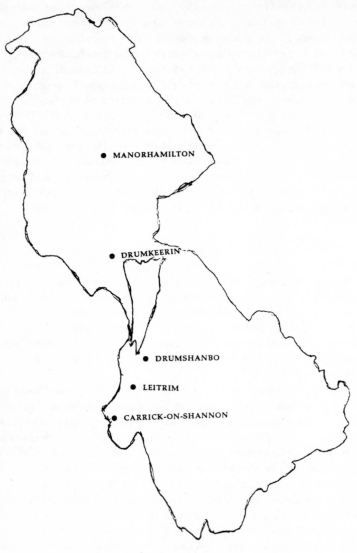

2. Map of Leitrim

were seven.[44] It is interesting to note that at the trial public houses were described as places of entertainment. Apart from grocery and hardware shops Drumkeerin also had a smithy, a fairgreen, market house, courthouse, post-office, a Protestant Church, a wheelwright's shop, a school and a barracks. An apothecary, who proved to be a key witness in the trial, also resided in the village. There was no water-pump in the parish or village. Water was provided by several spring-wells – three in particular were used by the villagers.[45]

THE PARISH ORGANISATIONS

During the 1820s a number of organisations were operating in the Drumkeerin area. These included the Steelboys; the Freemasons; the Orange Order; the Catholic Church and the Protestant Church. All of these, either through their activities or by reason of their membership were associated with the events of the trial.

The Steelboys were a Catholic, oath-bound secret society concerned with agitating for lower rents and at the time under discussion here, with mobilising opposition against sections of the Protestant community. They were accused of a number of crimes against supporters of the McGarrahans in the aftermath of the trial. Police reports suggest that the Steelboys were both numerous and powerful. In a letter dated 31 December 1826, the chief constable of the district, Daniel Winslow stated, 'I continue to receive reports of many people being sworn in and of nightly meetings. In one instance a man came and told me a person tendered to him an illegal oath and made an affidavit to that effect but has since evaded pointing out the individual so as to have him apprehended'.[46] Steelboy intimidation of the Protestant rector of Inishmagrath, which included burning his barn and sending him a 'violent threatening notice', persuaded him to give a rent-reduction of five shillings in the £, which was the amount demanded.[47] On another occasion when he attempted another rent adjustment the under-sashes of his windows were destroyed.[48] Punishments meted out by the Steelboys included beating with heavy sticks, whipping with leather thongs and carding. Carding was a process whereby the victim's flesh was scored by a sharp instrument such as an awl and then salt was poured into the wounds. As a rule the person's back was carded but in severe cases the face was chosen for mutilation. The Steelboys used fire arms occasionally especially when murder was their objective. Their attacks usually took place during the hours of darkness and often when their victims were in bed.[49]

Three murders were committed in the Drumkeerin area between Easter Monday and the end of June 1827, prompting the chief constable to inform his superior that 'I cannot too strongly recommend to your notice the state of this part of this barony and the necessity there is of something being done'.[50] Although the Steelboys were not openly accused of these murders, it may be implied from the following comment of Winslow that this illegal organisation was the most potent threat to peace in the area – 'Such is the state of the country ... that those who are not *combined* are afraid of being themselves murdered'. He added that wrongdoers could easily conceal themselves in the mountain caves and that crimes 'of a less violent nature are past number'.[51] In an obvious reference to a faction fight Winslow wrote that a dispute over the seating arrangements in a local church would be resolved 'in two battles on the successive Sundays in the presence of the priest'.[52]

In 1835 there were twenty-nine orange lodges in county Leitrim.[53] However there is no information on their location or membership. Two pieces of evidence, however, from the Maguire/McGarrahan case suggest that there was a lodge in Drumkeerin. Anne McGarrahan told the defence counsel that her father, Batty, was a member of the Orange Order.[54] A second reference relates how Batty was forced to employ Orangemen to dig his potatoes in the autumn of 1827.[55]

The warrant for Freemason Lodge 919 was granted to Drumkeerin in 1811 and between this date and the end of 1827 the names of seventy-eight members, Catholic and Protestant are recorded.[56] For a time in the 1820s the lodge held its meetings in Batty McGarrahan's Inn. Batty had been accepted as a member in 1819.[57] At this period there is no indication of Catholic clerical opposition to the organization. In 1831 the warrant was removed but in 1847 a new one was granted and Energy Lodge 187 was established. The local parish priest immediately objected to members of his flock joining the lodge on the grounds that it was 'love of orangeism makes the Protestant, love for ribbonism makes the Catholic join the Freemasons' and that 'it is my duty to discountenance all secret societies'.[58] Despite clerical opposition, Brother Francis Rogan, a farmer and practising Catholic, was elected Worshipful Master of the lodge in 1851. Rogan accused his parish priest of knowing 'nothing of a society where all religious distinctions are buried and where nothing but peace, harmony and brotherly love prevails'.[59] In 1824 James McGourty joined the lodge . McGourty was almost certainly the Catholic curate's brother and another key witness in the trial. In 1825 he was appointed junior warden of the lodge and for a time acted as secretary.[60] He appears to have left the parish by 1833 since the name McGourty does not appear in the Inishmagrath tithe applotment book for that year.

It is difficult to assess the influence of the Freemasons in Drumkeerin. The fact that Batty McGarrahan fell into bankruptcy and spent a term in the debtors' prison may indicate that their influence was slight. On the other hand, masons who were intending to emigrate were anxious 'to be recommended to all honest and worthy brothers around the globe' and carried letters of introduction from the local lodge. Among these was Hugh Kelly, who emigrated to England in 1822. He may have been the Hugh Bernard Kelly who was brought back from Manchester to give evidence for the defence at the trial.[61] Not all Protestants in the Drumkeerin area were members of the lodge. For example the names of two Protestant shopkeepers in the village, Miller and Milliken, do not appear in the register. Another Freemason lodge, 233, operated in Shivdillagh in the next parish of Killargy just two and a half miles from Drumkeerin village.[62] Perhaps the most significant aspect of Freemasonry in

3. Reverend Thomas Maguire

Drumkeerin was, that at a time of religious tension, in a small community, Catholics and Protestants were members of the same organisation.

THE CHURCHES AND THE RELIGIOUS DIVIDE

The only Catholic Church in the parish in 1827 was known locally as the Bogchapel, possibly from the name of the area – Baile na Móna – in which it was located. A thatched church, built in 1770, it was situated about one mile from the village. Its measurements were as follows: transept, sixty feet by

4. Anne McGarrahan

twenty feet – nave, forty-five feet by fourteen feet.[63] In the year 1852 it had a gallery but whether this was a later addition is not known.[64]

The Protestant church was consecrated five years after the building of the Bogchapel. The rector, Rev Russell Knox, the only Protestant clergyman in the parish was sixty-eight at the time of the trial.[65] A man of 'very eccentric and retired habits' he lived alone in a big rambling house about three miles from Drumkeerin.[66] Although only built in 1815 at a cost of £850[67] it was considered by Anne McGarrahan to be 'haunted'.[68] Knox was apparently a widower in 1827, whose family had all left the area. He had no servants except a steward who conducted the business of the estate. All of his near neighbours were Catholics.[69] The Glebe which lay 'immediately about the house' amounted to 540 acres of 'profitable land'.[70] Occasionally Anne McGarrahan was sent for when Mr Knox had visitors or when certain 'respectable families' called.[71] It is not clear what her function was on these occasions – possibly she was asked to prepare meals for the guests.

In 1834 services were held in the Bogchapel once every Sunday and on holydays. The average attendance was 2,500. In contrast the average attendance at Church of Ireland services was sixty. In 1834 the total number of Catholics was 7,827. Established Church members numbered 454.[72] The number of Protestant families in the parish in 1766 was five – the Catholic families numbered 574.[73] In 1826, three of the eight schools in the parish had Protestant teachers. One of these was the parish school which was presided over by the only female teacher in the parish, Mary Ovens. Two schools were financially supported by the London Hibernian Society and one by the Baptist Society. In another school the teacher 'was a Roman Catholic now a Protestant.'[74]

Although no accurate figures are available for the parish in the 1820s, it is certainly true that Protestants made up a very small minority in Inishmagrath. The isolation and insecurity of their position is typified by the request of the rector Mr. Knox to allow a policeman to stay overnight in his house after the window sashes had been destroyed. Incidentally the chief constable acceded to the request. That a large section of the Protestant community lived in the village of Drumkeerin, and were engaged in business there, may be inferred from a threatening notice posted on the door of the Bogchapel on Sunday May 13th 1827 ... 'we give this timely notice to all Catholics for the time to come to avoid buying any commodity whatever from the Protestants of Drumkeerin ... However there are two Protestants in Drumkeerin to be exempt from the above exclusion of commercial intercourse, namely Mr James Miller and Mr Thomas Milliken, they are liberal Protestants'. However Milliken did not escape the conflict between the two communities in December 1827. This particular notice which was posted on the chapel door resulted from 'the attack made on the character of our worthy and much to be respected parish priest [Rev T. McGuire]'. The background to the 'attack' was given in a letter sent by the chief constable to his superior officer Major Warbuton, Inspector General of Police.

Manorhamilton,
May 14th, 1827

Dear Sir,

I have the honour to enclose a copy of a notice which has been posted on the Chapel of the Parish of Inishmagrath yesterday. Subconstable Burke, stationed at Drumkeerin, on going to prayers took down the notice.

In explanation of that part which alludes to the attack on the character of Revd Thomas Maguire – a report has been circulated that a young girl daughter to the innkeeper at Drumkeerin who left home much the same time he did, has gone off with him. In giving this explanation I beg to say I know nothing of this except that the report was raised and should be sorry that my mentioning of it would be considered in anyway confirming the report.[75]

Seven months later Rev Thomas Maguire stood trial for the seduction of the innkeeper's daughter, Anne McGarrahan.

The Trial

Many of the tensions which operated in Ireland and in Leitrim came to a head in the trial of Rev Thomas Maguire for the seduction of Anne McGarrahan in 1827. He was a Catholic priest, she a Protestant. Maguire who was son of Thomas Maguire and Judith neé Maguire, of Tiroogan, parish of Kinawley, county Fermanagh was thirty-five years of age in the year of the trial. Educated in Maynooth College, he was ordained in 1816 by the bishop of Kilmore, Farrell O'Reilly, assisted by the bishop of Ardagh, James Magauran. His first appointment was as curate in Templeport, county Cavan. In 1818, the same year in which his uncle Patrick Maguire became coadjutor bishop of Kilmore, he was appointed parish priest of Drumreilly Lower and in February 1825 he was transferred to Drumkeerin, county Leitrim.[1] There was one other priest in Drumkeerin, the curate Patrick McGourty,[2] who was a year older than his parish priest and with whom Maguire had a very stormy relationship. According to McGourty's brother James, the two priests had quarrelled over payment of money covering the period when Maguire was away from his parish during the debate with Rev Richard Pope. Maguire referred to his curate as 'Dunderhead'.[3] Two servants, Quinn a man-servant and Mary Reynolds a maid were in Maguire's employment. His house was situated about two miles from Drumkeerin village and less than a mile from his church. He owned a carriage and was frequently seen 'driving through the village'.[4] A fluent Irish speaker, he, on one occasion delighted the historian Richard Madden, with a rendition of the famous Gaelic poem *An Bonnán Buí* in the original Irish and also in its English translation.[5] He was on friendly terms with a minor Gaelic poet, Tadhg Ó Floinn, who lived in an adjacent townland. Ó Floinn referred to him in one of his poems as 'an leon craosach Maguidhir' or 'The devouring lion Maguire'.[6]

Rev Maguire was a tall, strongly-built man. 'A quick blue eye, a nose slightly turned up, a heavy brow, a complexion of rustic ruddiness and thick lips which were better formed for rude disdain than for polished sarcasm were his characteristics.' He loved to tell anecdotes and his hobbies included coursing and game shooting and he excelled at the game of quoit. He was an able horseman, daring and stylish. His oratory was described as unornamented but 'he was a master of vigorous reasoning which was intelligible to all classes and startlingly conclusive … hearers of the humblest class could follow him'.[7]

Anne McGarrahan was twenty three in 1827. She was of slight build, of genteel appearance, not particularly handsome, intelligent and 'possessed a more cultivated mind than is generally supposed to belong to persons of her rank in life'.[8] She worked in her father's inn doing the household chores and occasionally assisted in the bar. She told the trial that 'I have lived in a public house since I was born'. Anne had a younger sister, Jane, and a brother Robert. Her mother and father, Batty were both alive at the time of the trial. In the course of the trial it emerged that she was a reader of books. She was complimented on her handwriting and she also had tried her hand at writing verse, particularly acrostics.[9]

On Thursday and Friday 13 and 14 December 1827 the seduction case was heard in the court of exchequer before Baron Sir William Cusack Smith and an all male jury comprised of Catholics and Protestants. According to the historian William O'Neill Daunt 'Smith as a judge was humane, considerate and painstaking. He went to the trouble of studying the Irish language in order to render himself independent of interpreters when witnesses were unable to speak English ... He supported the Catholic claims in 1795, but ... he considered that the preservation of the State Church Establishment ... should be carefully provided for in any measure of Catholic concession'.[10] During the trial, Smith kept on the bench a bottle of lavender water, to which 'I confess I was obliged occasionally to resort'.[11]

John Henry North, a man of middle height and aristocratic bearing, was the principal counsel for Batty McGarrahan. He was member of parliament for Plympton-Earl 1824–26. In his maiden speech in the house of commons he defended the Kildare Place Society and attacked the Irish Catholic clergy for obstructing its efforts.[12] North lived next door to Daniel O'Connell in Merrion Square, Dublin.[13] The other members of the McGarrahan legal team were, George Bennett, J.D. Jackson and Richard Keating with R.D. Meredith, solicitor.

The Catholic leader Daniel O'Connell, who had failed in his attempt to have the case heard outside the city of Dublin, was the leading counsel for the defence.[14] According to the author J. Roderick O Flanagan, this case was one in which O'Connell 'felt an amount of anxiety greater than counsel usually experience'.[15] He was also faced with the Trench libel case, which had received a preliminary hearing in the court of exchequer in late November.[16] O'Connell's team comprised the diminutive Richard Lalor Sheil, 'the horsehair wig covering not only his head but also his shoulders';[17] Dominic Ronayne,[18] Michael O'Loughlin[19] and J.P. Gahan with J. Fawcett, solicitor.

Rev Maguire was in the courtroom early, arriving at 10.30 a.m. The case commenced when the presiding judge took his seat at 12 noon. According to a newspaper report 'the hall and avenues to the courts were crowded by a vast assemblage at an early hour on Thursday morning. It would be impossible to convey any adequate idea of the anxiety which was to pervade all classes upon the subject of the trial. Every exertion was made by the city sub-sheriff, Mr Fearon to accommodate the public as far as the extent of the court permitted.'[20] Among the crowd were supporters of Maguire who had made the 120 mile journey from Drumkeerin.[21]

Junior Counsel for the prosecution, Richard Keating[22] introduced the case as follows:

> In this case, my Lord, Bartholomew McGarrahan is the plaintiff and the Rev Thomas Maguire is the defendant. This is an action on the case of seduction. The declaration contains four counts. The first count states that the defendant, intending to deprive the plaintiff of the service and assistance of his daughter and servant Anne McGarrahan, debauched and carnally knew her, whereby the said Anne McGarrahan became pregnant, and the plaintiff was deprived of the services of his said daughter, and was put to great expense in taking care of her. The second count is for the loss of her service omitting the expenses. The third count states that she was the servant of the plaintiff. The fourth count is the same as the first, omitting to state that she was his daughter. The damages are laid at £500. To this declaration the defendant has put in two pleas − first the general issue; secondly, that the plaintiff was discharged as an insolvent, and assigned all his effects, whereby his right and title to the supposed cause of action became vested in his assignee.[23]

George Bennett, a native of Cork, outlined the case for the prosecution. He was fifty years old, six feet tall, 'with an unaffected manner'.[24] He told the court that Rev Maguire had been appointed to the parish of Inishmagrath in county Leitrim in 1825 and

> ... having no suitable residence of his own he went to the plaintiff's inn, and resided for six weeks without intermission ... in September 1826 the plaintiff met with one of those misfortunes which will sometimes happen to the best of mankind: he was arrested for debt and thrown into gaol ... about the time he was in prison the seduction of his daughter was accomplished by the defendant. The consequence of this intercourse was that she became pregnant. In the month of March 1827, it was most likely that the appearance of this young woman must attract the notice of her family; the only persons aware of her situation were the defendant and herself ... Mr Maguire having found that she was in this predicament was driven to some difficulty; and the plan which he adopted was that she go to England ... She went to Liverpool and then to Manchester ... where she remained until the 2 July when she was delivered of a still-born child.

According to the prosecution, Anne McGarrahan left Manchester on 25 July 1827 and on her return to Drumkeerin she and her family decided to sue

Maguire. In the month of September Anne and her sister had a number of inter-
views with the priest. These continued into October but ended when 'she
would not come to his terms by accepting a sum of money, and he would not
come to hers by giving a legal private marriage'.[25]

Bennett was well into his speech when the proceedings were interrupted
by a loud noise in the hall. 'Shortly after, the witnesses for the prosecution
entered the court and at the request of the Counsel were accommodated with
seats in the chamber ... then there was tremendous shouting in the hall. It appears this tumult arose in consequence of the prosecutor's daughter being
brought through the vast body of persons who were assembled outside, on her
way to the court'.[26]

The trial was memorable for the powerful arguments presented by the defence in refutation of the allegations against Maguire. O'Connell's strategy was
threefold: to portray Anne as the village prostitute and a liar; to hammer home
the point that the McGarrahans were in dire financial straits and that they had
succumbed to the temptation of pecuniary gain; and to convince the jury that
the whole business was a conspiracy to discredit Maguire who had gained
national recognition by his victory over Pope.

The first witness for the prosecution was Anne McGarrahan herself. She
came to the witness table 'with much self-possession' expensively dressed in a
purple bombazine gown, a pelerine and a silk-lined, leghorn bonnet which
was 'shaped like a meal scoop'. She wore 'neat' gloves and carried a reticule.[27]
Joseph Devonsher Jackson,[28] one of the leading barristers of the period, led
her through her evidence. She told him that Maguire had married her in a
private ceremony sometime in September or October 1826. The ceremony,
at which there were no witnesses present, took place in a room of her father's
public house. She detailed the events in her life from the time she left
Drumkeerin in March 1827 to her return the following July. Particular points
on which she was questioned closely later by the defence included: her stay in
Woodfield, Boyle, the residence of her relation by marriage, Captain John
Dillon; the time she spent in England and the delivery of her child at 104, St.
George's Road, Manchester; her return home when she came as a deck pas-
senger from Liverpool to Dublin, then by canal boat to Longford and the rest
of the journey to Drumkeerin (about thirty-six miles) on foot. Anne was
cross-examined by Daniel O'Connell. He questioned her closely on the cost
of her apparel.

> *O'Connell*: What did that bonnet you wear cost?
> *Anne*:   Mr Maguire can best inform you.
> *O'Connell*: O it was a present of his.
> *Anne*:   It was.
> *O'Connell*: Was the veil?
> *Anne*:   No; that is my own.

O'Connell:	What did it cost?
Anne:	Upwards of a pound.
O'Connell:	The pelerine?
Anne:	It is my own.
O'Connell:	Who gave it to you?
Anne:	My mother.
O'Connell:	What did it cost?
Anne:	Nineteen shillings, two years ago.
O'Connell:	Did your sister go to Sligo to buy clothes for the trial?
Anne:	She did.
O'Connell:	She carried money with her.
Anne:	Yes.
O'Connell:	How much?
Anne:	Six pounds.
O'Connell:	Where was it got?
Anne:	It was a bill due by Mr Seeley – He paid his bill, remark.

According to Anne, after she left Drumkeerin in March 1826, she went to Woodfield, Boyle, county Roscommon, the residence of Captain John Dillon, who was later called as a defence witness. With reference to her time spent with the Dillons Anne was questioned as follows:

O'Connell:	When at Captain Dillon's with whom did you sleep?
Anne:	I slept with Miss Dillon.
O'Connell:	Did she know you were pregnant?
Anne:	I believe she did not.
O'Connell:	You had no reason to think she did?
Anne:	No! I did not confide it to her.
O'Connell:	You were six months gone with child then?
Anne:	I cannot say I was so much, I think I was not.
O'Connell:	How many nights did you sleep with Miss Dillon.
Anne:	Nine or ten nights.
O'Connell:	You had a wide bed?
Anne:	No, a narrow one.
O'Connell:	Who helped you to dress?
Anne:	Miss Dillon was kind enough to lace my stays.
O'Connell:	Did she never express any suspicions?
Anne:	Never directly.

Two specific pieces of information which came to light during Anne's cross-examination were crucial for the outcome of the case. One emerged during the following exchange between herself and O'Connell:

O'Connell: Did you not deny the charge against Mr Maguire?
Anne: I denied the charge; I denied that there was anything be-
               tween us but the facts are true.
O'Connell: Did you ever take a false oath about the business?
Anne: Not that I recollect.
O'Connell: Great God! Is that a thing you could have forgotten?
Anne: I believe I did not; I'm sure I did not.
O'Connell: O I see I have wound you up. Perhaps then you will tell me
               now, did you swear that it was false?
Anne: I never offered to swear but I said I would swear.

This reply provoked much laughter in the courtroom and J.D. Jackson for the
prosecution interjected.

Jackson: My Lord, this is not fair – I must –
O'Connell: I know what it is to protect a witness under cross–exami-
               nation. If it is ludicrous whose fault is it?

O'Connell persisted with this particular line of questioning.

O'Connell: Where was it you said the defendant was innocent?
Anne: I can't say where it was.
O'Connell: To whom do you think you denied it in England.
Anne: I think to the labourers who came over to work in England.

The second turning-point in the trial was the production by O'Connell of a
letter in Anne's handwriting and dated September 1827 which she said Rev
Maguire had dictated to her.

Dear Mr Maguire,

This is a precious moment indeed, the first I have had alone since my
illfated arrival. A secret friend has supplied me with pen, ink and paper
– but to the point – I am the innocent cause of your present persecution:
the Protestants hate and fear you, therefore, would they sacrifice my
honour and character to destroy yours: now mark well my words: be
advised by me and we will defeat them – is there a magistrate in this
county you can safely rely upon: if there is let him call here as it were
on a journey to feed his horse: let him have a strong affidavit of your innocence in his pocket, let me in the mean while know his name, that
I may have a lookout for him, and while his horse is feeding I will slip
downstairs and swear to the contents – I have already sworn to the same
effect but not before a magistrate. The moment you produce this affi-

davit you can publish it in the papers, and thus extinguish forever this diabolical conspiracy. £600 have been offered to our family to prosecute you, but money shall never corrupt my heart: the visits of gentlemen, their letters and promises to my poor father and mother, and Jane, have almost induced them to believe that it would be an act of virtue to punish a Jesuit Priest, but your innocence and my principals are your best safeguard: believe me Mr Maguire, that however humble my lot, my very soul sickens at the thought of willful perjury. I have a soul above sordid gain, put it to the test quickly. I know I will be turned out of doors – will you or the Catholics protect me? if not God will: I require not a pledge for the discharge of a sacred duty.

Dear Mr Maguire,

Your afflicted friend, A. McGarrahan

Asked again by O'Connell why she had written this letter McGarrahan repeated that she had done so at the dictation of Maguire. Her counsel J.D. Jackson asked her to explain the circumstances of the writing of the letter. She replied as follows: 'I went to Mr Maguire; he offered me money; I refused it; he asked me to write this letter which he had ready prepared on the table – ready written. He asked me –'. At this point she broke off and turning to Maguire she shouted 'O you villain! you villain!'. Then turning back to the court she said 'The bishop was there and, he Maguire, swore three solemn oaths on a German work, out of which he said he confuted Pope, that he would not disclose the circumstances.'

O'Connell devoted a large part of his cross-examination to an attempt at establishing that McGarrahan had had sexual relations with a number of men including Captain Berkley, from whom she had received a pair of gold earrings, Lieutenant Armstrong, Patrick Kearney, H.B. Kelly, Barrister Dixon and James McGourty brother of Rev Maguire's curate in Innishmagrath. She denied all charges of sexual intimacy. O'Connell's questions regarding the expense of the trial and the Orange Order produced the following exchange:

O'Connell: Pray did your father belong to any secret society?
Anne: I heard he was a freemason.
O'Connell: Was he anything else – an orangeman?
Anne: Yes.
O'Connell: Did you ever hear of a purple marksman?
Anne: Never.
O'Connell: Did you ever hear it explained from your father's lodge?
Anne: Never. I know my father was a freemason and I heard him say he was an orangeman.
O'Connell: If you heard it from you father would you believe it?

Anne:	I ought to believe his words.
O'Connell:	Do orangemen love the priests much?
Anne:	I don't know.
O'Connell:	Did you ever state in England that an orange conspiracy existed against the defendant?
Anne:	Never. Kelly told me so.
O'Connell:	And you did not tell him?
Anne:	I never did.
O'Connell:	Who is to pay the expenses of this action?
Anne:	My friends I believe.
O'Connell:	Who were those friends or friendly brothers?
Anne:	My Uncle Stewart is one of them.
O'Connell:	What is he?
Anne:	He is a farmer.
O'Connell:	And is he a very rich man?
Anne:	He is not considered rich.
O'Connell:	And who are the other contributing friends?
Anne:	I don't know.
O'Connell:	Do you know the precise sum he gave to support the action?
Anne:	I do not.
O'Connell:	Have you heard it?
Anne:	I did not.
O'Connell:	Or how much – from £1 to £1000?
Anne:	No.
O'Connell:	Where have you lived since you came to Dublin?
Anne:	In Mecklenburgh St. and in Mabbutt St.[29]

Three other witnesses were produced by the prosecution: Jane McGarrahan, aged twenty one, Anne's sister; Catherine McGarrahan, Anne's cousin; and Philip Dixon, a former editor of the *Irish Times* newspaper. Jane corroborated much of Anne's evidence adding that Maguire had told her that he wanted to send Anne extra money when she was in England but 'he was so closely watched while in Dublin by Coyne and Lawless, that he had not a minute to spare; Sir Edward Lees intimated that every letter to and from him was inspected in the Post-Office'.[30] Catherine McGarrahan's evidence was extremely important for the prosecution because she was the only one of the English-based witnesses who said that Anne was pregnant. She also said that she herself had assisted at the birth of Anne's still-born child. She was cross-examined by Richard Sheil:

Sheil:	Tell me Kitty what brought you to Manchester first?
Catherine:	To provide a living.
Sheil:	For yourself and child Kitty?

Catherine:	For myself only.
Sheil:	They live better in Manchester than in Leitrim. When did you go to Manchester?
Catherine:	In Whitsun week.
Sheil:	Where did you live before you went there?
Catherine:	I was servant in Mr McGarrahan's house and went with a family.
Sheil:	What family?
Catherine:	Mr George Stewart; he had a wife and five children; and she died shortly after they went over.
Sheil:	How many bedrooms were in the house?
Catherine:	They had but two bedrooms and a sitting parlour.
Sheil:	Where did you sleep – in the sitting room I suppose?
Catherine:	No, I slept with his eldest daughter.
Sheil:	Where did she sleep?
Catherine:	She slept in the same room with George Stewart.
Sheil:	When your cousin Anne came over where did she sleep?
Catherine:	She slept in the same room from Saturday to Tuesday.
Sheil:	Then you all slept in the one room?
Catherine:	We did. I afterwards got a lodging for her.
Sheil:	How many beds were in the room?
Catherine:	But two beds; one at each end.
Sheil:	Why, my Lancashire witch, do you mean to say the whole family, yourself, and the visitor, all slept in the one room?
Catherine:	Three of the children were dead; the eldest daughter, Miss McGarrahan, and I, slept together.
Sheil:	What! Three in a bed?
Catherine:	Well, it was a pretty sized bed and room for three in it.
Sheil:	Where do you live now?
Catherine:	At Drumkeerin before I came to town.
Sheil:	What wages had you from McGarrahan?
Catherine:	I had no wages before I went to Manchester.
Sheil:	Where do you live now?
Catherine:	Well I live at this moment in the Courthouse.
Sheil:	Oh! you are witty. What street in Dublin do you live in?
Catherine:	Well then I don't know, nor the house?
Sheil:	Where did you get that bonnet and shawl?
Catherine:	I borrowed the shawl from a neighbour and the bonnet is my own.
Sheil:	What wages were you to get on your return to McGarrahans?
Catherine:	I was promised eight shillings a quarter.[31]

The evidence of Philip Dixon pertained to three letters which the prosecution said were written to Anne by Maguire after she returned to Ireland.

The defence claimed they were forgeries. Dixon said one of them was in Maguire's hand and that 'the others appear to be written in a disguised hand but I can still perceive in them particular marks which lead me to believe they are in his handwriting'.[32]

The first day's proceedings concluded with O'Connell's address to the jury. He spoke for three hours. In a reference to the speech he wrote to his wife Mary: 'My heart is light, for all the Bar declare that your husband made the best speech he ever made. The Bar applauded at the end of my speech. They were silent when Mr North concluded'.[33]

O'Connell emphasised over and over again the points he had made in the course of his cross-examination. He heaped contempt on Batty McGarrahan, the 'pauper plaintiff' who although 'so latterly swore that his effects amounted only to 9s 6d ... has been able to have three of His Majesty's learned counsel and one who is equally learned ... Here we find an action brought at an enormous expense which cannot be less than £300'.

O'Connell labelled Anne McGarrahan 'a vile prostitute ... the strumpet of fifty paramours ... familiar with the rude and rapid progress of village prostitution' and without mentioning names he said that the 'diabolical' conspiracy was the concoction of 'the low wretches of the orange faction in Leitrim' and he asked the jury if they were 'prepared to minister to the vile orange lodges, who would gloat over their triumph'. He concluded his address with the following words –

> Gentlemen, I draw to a conclusion. I have redeemed my pledge; I have shown you that this action is not brought by the plaintiff ... it is a party action. Its object is a cold-blooded assassination, the safe and excruciating murder of high character ... and whom has it assailed? him, who at the altar of that high God who shall judge both you and him, has sworn to perpetual and unbroken chastity ... To you, Gentlemen, my client entrusts his case and into your box he throws his character – a character dearer to him than life. Can you believe that he has sacrificed his character ... can you believe that he stooped from his heavenly feast to feed on such wretched carrion as Anne McGarrahan? What beauty, what fascination is there about her? How vulgar in her association and made superior to those associated by that species of education, which ... enabled her to conceive and execute this odious plan of false accusation. It is your interest as men to discountenance falsehood and perjury – as Christians you are under a sacred obligation to crush and trample underfoot this diabolical conspiracy.[34]

Rev Thomas Maguire attended the court both days of the trial. The fact that he was not requested to take the stand as a witness for the defence, was not referred to by the prosecution at any time during the proceedings.

SECOND DAY, FRIDAY 14 DECEMBER 1827

It was during the evidence given by the first witness for the defence, Hugh Bernard Kelly that the names of John Duckworth and Charles Cox came up in connection with the action. Kelly, a schoolmaster in Liverpool and formerly a grocer in Drumkeerin, told the court that Anne McGarrahan had said in July 1827 when she returned to Ireland that the allegations against Rev Maguire were 'all a parcel of prejudice, and a conspiracy set on foot by her uncle Willie Stewart, Parson Johnson, Mr Cox, Mr Duckworth and others whose names I do not recollect'. Kelly also said that before he went to England in 1822 he had sexual relations with Anne. If this statement was true and if the 'criminal connexion' took place as he said, before his own marriage in 1821, then Anne was at most seventeen years of age when she slept with Kelly. During a visit to Drumkeerin in early July 1827 Kelly had gone to see the McGarrahans who told him they knew nothing of Anne's whereabouts. Kelly also called on Rev. Maguire 'to return him a vote of thanks for his recent exertions in the Discussion' on behalf of the St. Patrick Society in Liverpool. Anne was brought back to the witness table to answer Kelly's allegations.

O'Connell:	Pray sit down Miss.
Anne:	I prefer standing Sir, if you please.
O'Connell:	I do not doubt it.
Bennett:	Do you know that man?
Anne:	I do.
Bennett:	Had you ever any criminal intercourse with him?
Anne:	So help me God, in the sight of your Lordship – in the sight of this honourable court and of High Heaven – I never had'. Then turning to Kelly she said, 'You are a perjured villain; you are a rascal'.
O'Connell:	Did you see him at Liverpool and Manchester?
Anne:	I did.
O'Connell:	Did you go to chapel with him?
Anne:	I went to see the Catholic school with him, but not the chapel. The school was under the chapel.
A juror:	Were you very ill in your confinement?
Anne:	The doctor said it was not a dangerous case, though I was ill enough.
A juror:	How long were you ill?
Anne:	From 10 o'clock on Sunday night to eight on Monday morning; the child was still born.
A juror:	Who attended you in your confinement?
Anne:	Doctor Hollwell.
A juror:	Did Kelly know anything about it?

Anne:	No.
A juror:	Did you walk all the way from Manchester?
Anne:	I walked part of the way and came the rest of the way on a wagon.[35]

Another witness, Patrick Prior, who knew the McGarrahans in Drumkeerin said that when he met Anne in Manchester, 'she had no more appearance of being with child than I have.' He added 'I even lent Anne McGarrahan some money to carry her home. I changed a sovereign and gave her ten shillings of it, so that I had no spite to her family'.[36]

James McGourty, the Drumkeerin curate's brother was aged twenty four at the time of the trial. He had been married two years previously. McGourty told the court that he was fond of amusement and sport and that he some-times hunted with Rev Maguire. Regarding his relationship with Anne he said 'I have been in company with Anne McGarrahan; I was often in company with her alone … Anne and I drank Scaltheen twice or three times together; on some of those occasions that I was with her I had criminal intercourse with her … after the criminal connexion she said, 'Now you know what you have done remark', 'I do', says I, and downstairs I went'.[37]

Captain John Dillon, a relation of the McGarrahan's caused a stir in the courtroom when he appeared for the defence. He seemed to be suffering from the effects of too much drink and his blunt answers were in contrast to the more circumspect replies of other witnesses. O'Connell asked him to describe a particular romantic encounter involving Anne McGarrahan and Lieutenant Armstrong which took place in the summer-house at the rear of the McGarrahan inn. Dillon said that he saw Anne lying on her back on the oval seat with Armstrong bending over, kissing her but 'by virtue of my oath I did not see his pantaloons down; I saw a rake break under her and that's all; the seat was too narrow'. He was cross-examined by J.D. Jackson.

Jackson:	Are you a married man?
Dillon:	I am, I was married in the year 1818.
Jackson:	Is your wife living?
Dillon:	I don't know.
Jackson:	Nor don't care?
Dillon:	No, I don't.

★   ★   ★

Jackson:	You often take a drop yourself?
Dillon:	Often.
Jackson:	A good large sup, I suppose.
Dillon:	Sometimes.
Jackson:	Are you quite sober now?
Dillon:	I think I am.

★ ★ ★

Jackson: Do you know a young lady of the name of Anne Dillon.
Dillon: I have not known her for several years.
Jackson: When you did know her you were very intimate?
Dillon: We were.
Jackson: I am told you found her soft?
Dillon: I do not know what you mean by asking me if I found her soft.
Jackson: By virtue of your oath did you not seduce her?
Dillon: By virtue of my oath I did.
Jackson: And she was your relative?
Dillon: She was.[38]

The evidence of Robert Lee, apothecary in Drumkeerin, established three important points for the defence. During a conversation he had with Anne in her father's parlour after her return from England she said she had left home as a result of a family dispute. She also told him that she never had sexual relations with Rev Maguire and that 'there were wonderful offers made to her with respect to this action; that these great offers were made to her to prosecute Mr Maguire'. Lee added that he was friendly with Batty McGarrahan and attended the family in a professional capacity. He concluded; 'what I have said I would not say if it was not to clear up Anne's character'.[39]

Three witnesses, including the well-known editor and journalist Frederick Conway, testified that letters alleged to be in Maguire's handwriting, were forgeries.[40]

One of the most intriguing aspects of the Maguire/McGarrahan episode was the role of Catherine McWeeney, a young girl who lived opposite the inn in Drumkeerin. According to the prosecution, Catherine brought letters from Maguire to Anne McGarrahan. However, although she was in Dublin for the case, brought up by the defence, she was not put on the stand. Each side, prosecution and defence, accused the other of not using her as a witness. John Henry North, in his concluding address, said that the defence 'triumphantly ask why we do not produce this woman. We may retort and ask them, why they do not produce her? We have traced her into a carriage with the servants of the defendant in this town. She has been brought up to support the defendant's case, and to support that case she would have been produced this day, were they not afraid that she could not stand the ordeal of a cross-examination'. Possibly each side considered that her evidence could do damage to both prosecution and defence. In any event on her return to Drumkeerin she was feted by the Maguire supporters.

Before the prosecution address to the jury, O'Connell presented to the court Batty McGarrahan's petition and schedule as an insolvent. The claim against him was for £94. His only return in the schedule was one pig, valued at 10 shillings and his cash assets amounted to 9 shillings and 6 pence. He swore in his petition that he had no servant.[41]

John Henry North in his final speech, addressed the major issues of the defence case. He dealt with the assertion that Anne was a woman of low morals by emphasising that if she was 'the romping prostitute' of the village, someone would have warned Maguire and he would not have stayed six weeks at the McGarrahan's inn. Kelly, McGourty, and Dillon, he described as disreputable characters whose evidence was unreliable. He made no reference to the apothecary Lee. His attempt to discredit the notion that the case amounted to a conspiracy against the priest relied on an appeal to the jury to reject such an extraordinary viewpoint. The fact that the names of Duckworth, Cox and others only emerged in evidence a short time before, gave North no chance to produce witnesses to counteract the conspiracy allegation. He concluded:

> No, Gentlemen of the Jury, this is neither a political or religious action. It has been raised indeed by the circumstances of the times and of the country to an unnatural importance; but it must be decided, like every other action, upon the weight of the evidence, and its own intrinsic merits.[42]

A newspaper reporter noted 'the distorted countenance, the convulsed limbs and the trembling frame of the Rev defendant during the splendid speech of Mr North'. [43]

The presiding judge, Sir William Smith began his address to the jury at 5pm and spoke for an hour and a half. He highlighted the September 1827 letter which the defence had produced in court. Smith implied that the evidence in this letter weakened the prosecution case. Towards the end of his speech he had this to say … 'neither can I see why Kelly and Lee and Prior and McGourty, and perhaps I should add Dillon – though we have his own word for the profligacy of his life – why the five shall all come forward to commit disinterested perjury. Perhaps they come forward thus; or, perhaps there lurks some interest which eludes detection'. [44]

The jury retired at 6.30 pm and returned at 7 pm with a verdict for the defendant with 6d costs.[45]

The Fall Out

'The Triumph of Rev Mr Maguire is complete. Victory crowned us with laurels, only think, the jade was not with child at all! We had a victory with the full approbation of the judge'.[1]

This private opinion on the trial, expressed by O'Connell in a letter to his wife Mary, conveys his sense of elation which was shared by Maguire's supporters as they massed outside the Four Courts to await the emergence of their hero.

After receiving the congratulations of his counsel and well-wishers, Maguire, together with James O'Gorman Mahon, a Catholic graduate of Trinity College, attempted to slip unnoticed out of the building. However they were recognized immediately and 'amidst the most deafening cheers', they were forced into one of the carriages at the gates. The horses were unharnessed and the carriage, escorted by the huge crowd, was drawn across Ormond Bridge to the nearby residence on Merchant's Quay of Nicholas Mahon, a prominent Catholic in the city. Maguire went upstairs and spoke to the people from the drawing-room window: 'My friends, I have been exposed to the ordeal and declared pure. Under God, I owe this result to my good cause, conducted by Daniel O'Connell and my other legal advisers, to the upright and enlightened judge and to an honest jury of fellow citizens. Such protection could only have sheltered me from the base and powerful conspiracy by which I was unprovokedly assailed'. He went on to say that he hoped that the protection he received would act as an incentive to dissuade his listeners from 'violating the laws of the land, even in the slightest degree'.[2] Maguire's pleas fell on deaf ears as his supporters went on the rampage in celebration of the victory. According to one account the crowd was:

> insolent, daring, ferocious and abandoned – a suborned assembly of the vilest ruffians that ever were disowned in any civilized community of pagans ... the metropolis of Ireland was hardly extensive enough for the exhibition of the beastly scenes by which it was disgraced on Friday night.

Windows which were not lit up for the victory were smashed. It was reported that one of the most brilliantly illuminated houses was 9, Mountjoy Square, the residence of Dr Daniel Murray, the Catholic archbishop.[3]

The riots were serious enough to warrant the calling out of the military to augment the police numbers. The dragoons used their swords to disperse the crowds and their conduct was deemed excessive by the *Morning Register* which cited a couple of examples of brutality —

> a cowardly ruffian dropped his sword in making a cut at the defenceless people in Francis Street. Another ruffian cut at a Catholic clergyman as he was peaceably walking along the street and did him, we are told, much injury.[4]

Most of the riots took place in the north of the city which 'exhibited a singular spectacle the following day in the prodigious number of ruined windows'. The windows of a hundred Protestant citizens were said to have been destroyed. Sackville Street sustained the most damage but one account hinted that enemies of Maguire, in an effort to discredit him, might have been responsible. The shop window of 4 Capel Street, the property of Maguire's friend and mentor Richard Coyne was also smashed.[5]

The day after the trial, Hugh Kelly, witness for the defence, in a letter to the *Morning Register*, took exception to North's description of him 'as a demon and monster yawned up from the lowest hell'. Kelly said that he had been subpoenaed to appear and also that 'the haughty orator' was aware that his act of sexual intercourse with Anne McGarrahan had taken place before his marriage.

Celebrations of Maguire's victory extended beyond Dublin. For example, a demonstration which took place in Roscommon town on 17 December was not welcomed by a correspondent of the *Roscommon and Leitrim Gazette*:

> Our town was in a state of confusion last night owing to an illumination for Maguire ('on his victory over the Protestants' as they ignorantly term it here). There were fiddles, fifes and other instruments playing through the town until a late hour. I am proud to say that our Protestant townsmen, save a few rotten members did not illuminate.[6]

One of the local papers, the *Sligo Journal*, which Maguire called 'the Western Rag', gave its views on the trial in an editorial:

> If the Roman Catholic Archbishop of Dublin had put his chapels in mourning for the frailties of his Rev brother instead of the triumphant howlings of the populace and the factious illumination of a whole city — it would have been a more suitable commentary.[7]

The balladeers also swung into action particularly on the Maguire side. The following extracts from a ninety-one line satire, '*The Nymphs of Drumkeerin or Love and Scaltheen*', which was composed immediately after the trial reflect the high emotions which the case engendered.

Rejoice, rejoice ye honest hearts
Pointless fell the envenomed darts
The base conspiracy is o'er
And infamy stamped upon a whore.

* * *

Alas, Alas! not North's great powers
Were he to speak for twenty hours
Nor Keating's classic eloquence
Could controvert plain common sense.

* * *

O'Connell hail!, triumphant chief
In every cause where justice claims relief
And thou, whose Ciceronian tongue
(And whose prized life may Heaven prolong)
Thou pride of Ireland Richard Sheil
Whose nervous words, whose strong appeal
Ne'er failed in virtue's glorious cause,
Accept a nation's warm applause.

* * *

This alias damsel, this steamboat tripper
Attached alike to mate and skipper
Source of Attraction and Detraction's source
Will e're thy conscience feel remorse?
Shoulds't thou outlive thy lovers all
Thy years in number won't be small;
McCann, Berkley, Lawyer Dixon,
McGourty, Palmer and old Nick's son,
Pat Carney, Seally, Kelly, fifty more
To whom you proved yourself a whore.[8]

Early in January 1828, Daniel O'Connell told a Catholic Association meeting that another Anne McGarrahan type case was about to happen in Cavan. This was also a case involving a priest, Rev Thomas Brady who was charged with the seduction of Mary Kenny, née Reilly. She claimed she had two children by the priest, one before and one after her marriage. During the trial, which took place in Cavan town the prosecution put the following question to a witness — 'Had you any further communication with Maguire about the child?' The blunder was immediately seized on by Richard Sheil defence counsel who commented: 'The coincidence is very natural – the altars of Leitrim are not very far from the the altars of Cavan'. The charge against Rev Brady was dismissed.[9]

LEITRIM

Was there a conspiracy against Maguire? If there was who were the leaders? Two of the most prominent personalities in the Second Reformation Movement in Leitrim, John Duckworth and Charles Cox were both named as conspirators in the trial. They both denied any involvement in letters published in the same issue of a local paper. The date of the letters is 24 December 1827 and both are remarkably similar in their wording. Duckworth claimed that he had never 'either directly or indirectly took any part in the prosecution of Mr Maguire, by subscription, advice or in any other way – nor was I asked for a subscription by any person to carry on the prosecution.' He added: 'In giving this contradiction, I beg it may be clearly understood that I offer no opinion on the merits or results of the trial'.[10] In the absence of documented evidence it is impossible to prove the conspiracy change. There remains however the question of the legal costs, a factor alluded to by Sir William Cusack Smith, the trial Judge, when a motion for a re-trial was mooted a few weeks later.[11]

On the night of 30/31 December 1827 a sixty yard long, meadow wall, five feet high, on Cox's property at Tullyleague, Carrick-on-Shannon was maliciously demolished by 'some evil disposed person or persons'. Cox was incensed enough to offer a reward of £10 for the apprehension of those responsible.[12]

That there was a widespread boycott of Protestant businesses in Leitrim in the weeks after the trial would seem to be borne out by the following notice posted on the door of Murhane Catholic church, Drumshanbo (about ten miles from Drumkeerin) on 10 February 1828

> Catholics not to buy goods from Protestants in Drumshanbo, particularly in Crawfords and Barrons … numerous Roman Catholics will follow the maxims set before them in neighbouring towns to prevent such friendly people from dealing in such bigots' shops.[13]

On 23 February 1828, the Protestant English-born manager of the Arigna mines (about seven miles from Drumkeerin) was shot dead, reputedly by the Steel Boys. His name, Charles Cox, caused confusion at the time. However, he was not related to Charles Cox of Carrick-on-Shannon. His death seems to have been the result of dispute over company funds. The *Roscommon and Leitrim Gazette* suggested that it might have been a case of mistaken identity and added – 'If some prompt measures be not resorted to by the Government, the lives of our fellow Protestants cannot be secure for a single night'.[14]

THE VILLAGE

'Had the injury come from any body of people with whom we were at vari-
ance it might be over looked; but to come from a people with whom we had
the most friendly intercourse is what we cannot pass over in silence'[15] – the
feelings of resentment towards the Protestant inhabitants of Drumkeerin, expressed in the threatening notice posted on the Bog Chapel the previous May,
translated into displays of triumphalism and incidents of revenge now that the
victory had been achieved. The Drumkeerin supporters of Rev Maguire cel-
ebrated his victory on the night of Christmas Eve 1827. Lights shone in the
village windows as a huge crowd led by the curate's brother James McGourty
assembled in front of McGarrahan's Inn shouting 'Maguire forever'. A shopkeeper gave out a large quantity of whiskey to the crowd and also provided
three tar-barrels for a bonfire. Catherine McWeeney, dressed in a new beaver
bonnet, new gown and boots, arrived by carriage in the village accompanied by
other girls. The horse was unharnessed and Catherine was put sitting beside the
driver. Then with a lighted lantern in each hand she was conveyed up and
down the single street. The police made an effort to preserve the peace but
later decided to return to the barracks and allow the celebration to continue.[16]

The next day, Maguire said the Christmas mass in his small thatched church.
He told the congregation that he had been vindicated and that 'he would get
possession of the two houses belonging to the McGarrahans'. Two days later,
a crowd led again by James McGourty gathered outside the McGarrahan's
inn.[17] Thomas Milliken, the shopkeeper who had been described as a liberal
Protestant seven months before, was made to pay the price for a neighbourly
act of his wife. Catherine McGarrahan had told the trial that the shawl she
was wearing had been lent to her by a neighbour. Local intelligence identified
the benefactor and goods which had been bought in Milliken's shop by the
country people were returned to him 'mangled and useless'. He approached
Rev Maguire with a plea to have him restored to the favour of his former
customers. His request was denied.[18]

Early in January 1828, the *Sligo Journal* reported that in the Drumkeerin
area there was 'a set of persons called the Steelboys, well armed, perpetrating
the greatest disorders – no person dare go into the house of the unfortunate
McGarrahan'. The Steelboys in the main, targeted McGarrahan relatives and
supporters for punishment. On 1 January they entered the house of an aged
man Hugh McGoldrick, who had once worked for Batty. McGoldrick was
not at home but his wife was carded. On the same date the house of John
Palmer, a relative of the McGarrahans, was set on fire. Another relative Pat
McGarrahan was beaten up a few days later. He tried to protect himself with
a graip but was dragged outside stark naked, doused over and over again with
cans of cold water and made to swear three oaths: that he would not conform
to the established church; that he would clear out of the district within eight

days and that he would not proceed with the prosecution of a man who had beaten him when he was returning from a funeral. Another incident involved a very young Protestant girl who was travelling 'from the upper part of Maguire's county' towards Manorhamilton to visit relations. She was attacked by 'half a dozen ruffians' but the driver succeeded in rescuing her when an attempt was made to drag her into a nearby house.[19]

The worst incident involving the Steelboys was the murder of a man named Cassidy on 10 January. Cassidy, who was accused of 'violating the laws of the Steelboys by dealing with a Protestant', was severely tortured before he died. After being whipped with a leather thong he was compelled to swallow tobacco and soap, which his attackers said had been bought in a Protestant shop. The *Sligo Journal* suggested that the murder was the work of 'Maguirites'. This was denied by Rev Maguire.[20]

THE FINAL ACT

On Saturday 2 February, in the court of exchequer, Mr K.D. Jackson moved to have the verdict in the Maguire/McGarrahan case set aside and thus open the way for a new trial. On the following Monday week four judges of the Court, Pennefeather, McClelland, O'Grady (the chief judge) and Smith who had presided at the December 1827 trial, gave their decisions at a public hearing. With the exception of Smith, the other three came down in favour of a retrial. Each of the three gave his own particular reasons for his decision, and the language used at some points by these legal luminaries affords an indication of their personal prejudices.

For example O'Grady referred to Hugh Kelly as 'a wretch, who being the teacher of youth – and a pretty moral kind of teacher he is – should have the unblushing effrontery to swear what he did swear in the trial'. The three judges who disagreed with Smith suggested that he had misdirected the jury. O'Grady put it like this:

> He first tells the jury that it was for them to say whether they attached credibility to the testimony of the witness [Anne McGarrahan]. Now could any man pronounce better charge than that? Baron Smith does not stop there; but having told the jury what they ought to do, he goes on and tells them if he were in the box he would not believe one word she swore. You see he first got an advantage over the jury by leaving them to themselves, and then he makes himself as it were a thirteenth juror, and being in the box with them, he says, 'never mind what I told you a while ago, but now that I am here snugly with you, I tell you what I would do – that is, not believe a single word she said.'[21]

Some members of the public found this amusing and Smith rose to his feet as if to leave the bench but then changed his mind.[22] Later, at a public sitting of the court of exchequer, O'Grady apologised to Smith for his remarks saying that 'he had in private assured Brother Smith that nothing offensive was intended and he had great pleasure in repeating that assurance from the Bench'. Richard Coyne published the full statement under the title *The Satisfactory Apology of the Right Hon. Standish O'Grady, Chief Baron*.[23]

Sir William Cusack Smith in his statement, which ran to over seventy pages, defended his handling of the trial and dealt with the main points raised by his fellow judges: his 'biased' address to the jury; the composition of the jury; the intimidation of the witnesses; the role of Catherine McWeeney and the evidence of Hugh Kelly. He also gave his opinion on the conspiracy theory and the proposed calling of new prosecution witnesses. 'As to misdirection', he said, 'I shall scarcely say anything ... I gave no direction and consequently could not have given any misdirection ... Thus I could only mislead the jury by a misrepresentation intentional or inadvert, of the facts ... If the Counsel on either side had found me mis-stating any fact, they would have suggested this, and set the matter right'.[24] Smith dismissed the charge that the jury had not been properly vetted by emphasising that no juror had been objected to by either Counsel and regarding the threatening of witnesses he said, 'As to any intimidation of witnesses or jurors, as I certainly was not frightened, why should I figure to myself that the jury were?'[25] Catherine McWeeney, he said, could have been subpoened to appear by the prosecution and in fact she was present in the court-room during the trial. Smith defended the key defence witness Hugh Bernard Kelly – 'It did appear that at the time of his alleged connection with Anne McGarrahan he was not married. Upon the evidence it might be so or it might not. Then again, he did not appear to have been a relation of her mother's – it was his wife that was so'.[26]

Smith commented on the prosecution's intention to call as a witness the doctor who allegedly had assisted at the delivery of Anne's still-born baby and the woman who provided the coffin – 'What could Hollwell prove, if able to identify Anne McGarrahan at all, but that she had been delivered of a still-born child for which Mrs Russell provided a coffin?'[27]

In his comment on O'Connell's assertion that the case was the result of a conspiracy, Smith seemed to incline to the view that Anne McGarrahan and her family were not acting alone:

> There may be consent with conspiracy ... but we must be blind and deaf and far gone in fatuity ... who can doubt that ... there is consent, encouragement and contribution. The cheerful countenance and presumably free disembursements of Mr Meridith [the prosecution lawyer] clearly indicate that he has no misgivings on the subject of his bill of costs. One cannot look even cursorily through the newspapers, without

seeing that there was more than the McGarrahan family who take a
lively interest in the action.'[28]

Smith stressed the fact that O'Connell had tried to have the case heard outside the city of Dublin, but 'the plaintiff prevailed. He had availed himself of
his legal privilege of bringing a transitory action in a county different from
that in which the cause of the action had really arisen ... Nothing but a city
of Dublin jury would content him'.[29]

In his concluding remarks Baron Smith was contemptuous of those who
sought to intimidate him:

> I may have been often wheedled, duped, and humbugged, into mea-
> sures; but I am not conscious of having ever suffered myself to be dra-
> gooned, and I will not, in my old days, begin to change my practice.
>
> I suppose I love my life, for it is natural for one to do so, but I hope I
> shall always love my conscience better.
>
> In the present case, it obliges me to withhold my assent from the propri-
> ety of interfering with this verdict. I do so with a deference and respect
> for the dissentient opinions of my Lord Chief Baron, and my brethren,
> as sincere (and it cannot be more so) as is my contempt for those who
> have presumed to question my integrity, or to calculate on my fears.[30]

The majority decision in favour of setting aside the verdict meant Rev
Maguire could be brought before the courts again. It was expected that moves
would be made to hold a new trial before the end of the law term in May.
This never happened and the *Roscommon and Leitrim Gazette* reported that
'Friday 16 May was the last day for serving notice of a trial ... up to 6 'clock
no notice had been served in the case'.[31]

Conclusion

The Maguire/McGarrahan case generated an enormous amount of interest and was absorbed into Drumkeerin folklore. The most enduring throwback to the trial is a ballad, still well-known in the district, which contains the following lines:

In famed Drumkeerin he lived contented
And preached the gospel that was taught of old,
Till a female Judas named Anne McGarrahan
Swore hard against him for the love of gold.[1]

Traditions associated with the case include a belief that Daniel O'Connell visited Drumkeerin in disguise to familiarize himself with the local situation[2] and that he persuaded James McGourty to swear he had sexual relations with Anne McGarrahan.[3] Another story tells that Maguire and Anne used to walk hand in hand on Corry Strand on the northern shore of Lough Allen but that 'it never went any further'.[4]

The days of the trial were an epoch in the history of the Drumkeerin area. Never again did it hit the national headlines nor its population experience an exposure to the public glare which for the majority meant triumph, for the minority failure and isolation. The trial revealed the tensions between two communities, the one relying on privilege, the other on numbers for dominance. Its story unveils vivid cameos of the social life of the time; an aged clergyman nervous in his rectory; a village 'illuminated' for victory; the curate's brother roaring in triumph outside the house of the vanquished and the activities associated with the only inn in the village.

When the conflict transferred to the metropolitan arena, it assumed a national significance involving leading political, legal and clerical personalities of the period and as Maguire's Drumkeerin supporters mingled with the vast crowds in and around the Four Courts they became participants in a bigger contest which had Daniel O'Connell, Richard Sheil and others as vital players. And central to the whole proceedings was their own priest from a remote rural parish in the north-west of Ireland.

Rev Thomas Maguire left Dublin with his status enhanced. His subsequent career was marked by frequent invitations to preach charity sermons all over the country. In Dublin, he preached in St. Francis' Church, Merchants Quay and St Theresa's Church, Clarendon Street.[5] On the occasion of the opening of a new church in Ballyshannon, county Donegal in 1835 he 'entered the chapel dressed most splendidly in white cambrick, tastefully embroidered and having taken his stand on the altar, commenced his sermon ...'[6] After a sermon he was usually perspiring freely and as a precaution against colds he used to plunge a red hot poker into a glass of whiskey and drink it down.[7]

Before he left Drumkeerin he built a second church and he did likewise in his next parish, Ballinamore.[8] In 1833 he published a book titled '*False Weights and Measures of the Protestant Curate of Cavan Examined and Exposed*'[9] – and five years later he was engaged in another public discussion in Dublin. Rev Tresham Gregg of Trinity College, was his opponent on this occasion.

> From the county Leitrim to Dublin city
> To meet Tresham Gregg he went all the way
> Where he confounded him where thousands gathered,
> With shame the preacher ran away.[10]

Rev Maguire continued to take an active role in politics. In December 1828 he attended a public dinner in Carrick-on-Shannon which was attended by the earl of Leitrim and other county gentry favourable to Catholic Emancipation. He was toasted as 'one of the old school, one of the Maguires of Tempo'.[11] He also discharged his debt to O'Connell by canvassing for him in the Clare election campaign, 1828.[12] The Trench libel case, which dragged on through much of 1828, was finally settled in the court of common pleas. Archbishop Trench was awarded £50 damages.[13]

On 2 December, 1847 Rev Maguire died unexpectedly. Six weeks later his body was exhumed after his brother and sister-in-law, who had lived with him, had been found to have died from arsenic poisoning. A quantity of arsenic was also found in Maguire's body.[14]

> The Rev gentleman is much lamented
> For his brother and sister-in-law they do deplore
> They fell a victim to death precarious
> By some deadly poison that remained in store.[15]

Anne McGarrahan disappeared from the public scene. According to tradition she went to Manchester and lived out her days there.[16]

Notes

THE RELIGIOUS CONFLICT

1 Fergus O'Ferrall, *Catholic Emancipation, Daniel O'Connell and the birth of Irish democracy 1820–1830* (Dublin 1985) p. 20.
2 Fergus O'Ferrall, *Catholic Emancipation*, p. 20.
3 *Roscommon and Leitrim Gazette*, 11 February 1826.
4 *Roscommon and Leitrim Gazette*, 11 December 1826.
5 I. Whelan, 'Edward Nangle and the Achill Mission 1834–1852' in Raymond Gillespie and Gerard Moran (eds), *A Various Country, Essays in Mayo History 1500–1900*, (Westport, 1987).
6 *Roscommon and Leitrim Gazette*, 20 October 1827.
7 *Roscommon and Leitrim Gazette*, 7 April 1827.
8 *Roscommon and Leitrim Gazette*, 5 January 1828.
9 *Roscommon and Leitrim Gazette*, 19 May 1827.
10 *Roscommon and Leitrim Gazette*, 26 May 1827.
11 *Roscommon and Leitrim Gazette*, 23 September 1827, 9 December 1827.
12 Donal Kerr, 'James Brown, Bishop of Kilmore', (1829–65) in *Breifne*, vi, no. 22 (1984) pp 109–154.
13 *Enniskillen Chronicle and Erne Packet*, 28 December 1826. *Roscommon and Leitrim Gazette*, 23, 30 December 1826.
14 Donal Kerr, 'James Brown', pp 109–154.
15 *Roscommon and Leitrim Gazette*, 21 January 1826.
16 Abraham, O'Conor, *Concord Lodge 854, Carrick-on-Shannon 1798–1897* p. 5 (Copy in Leitrim county Library)
17 *Roscommon and Leitrim Gazette*, 28 January 1826.
18 *Roscommon and Leitrim Gazette*, 20 January 1827.
19 *Roscommon and Leitrim Gazette*, 11 February 1826.
20 *Roscommon and Leitrim Gazette*, 13 May 1826.
21 *Roscommon and Leitrim Gazette*, 18 November 1826.
22 *Roscommon and Leitrim Gazette*, 20 January 1827.
23 *Roscommon and Leitrim Gazette*, 30 December 1826.
24 *Roscommon and Leitrim Gazette*, 5 May 1827.
25 *Roscommon and Leitrim Gazette*, 12 May 1827; Rev Terence, O'Rorke, *The History of Sligo Town and County*, (2 vols, reprint Sligo, 1986) i, pp 345–46.
26 *Authenticated Report of the Discussion which took place between the Rev Richard Pope and Rev Thomas Maguire: in the Lecture Room of the Dublin Institute on 19th, 20th, 21st, 23rd, 24th and 25th of April 1827*. (Dublin R. Coyne, Capel St, R.M. Tims, Grafton St and W. Curry, Jun and county Sackville St.)
27 *Authenticated Report of the Discussion* ... April 17th ... p. 6.
28 W. J. Fitzpatrick, *The Life, Times and Correspondence of the Right Rev Dr Doyle, Bishop of Kildare and Leighlin*, (Dublin, 1861), p. 33.

29 Thomas Wall: *The Sign of Dr Hay's Head*, (Dublin, 1958), pp 64–65.

30 *Roscommon and Leitrim Gazette*, 28 April 1827.

31 Trinity College, Dublin Ms N 5 27.

32 Desmond Bowen, *The Protestant crusade in Ireland, 1800–1870*. (Dublin, 1978) p. 107.

33 W.J. Fitzpatrick, *The Life, Times and Correspondence of the Right Rev ...* 1861, p. 33.

34 *Report of the trial in the case of Barw. M'Garahan versus the Rev T. Maguire before Baron Smith and a special Jury*, (Dublin, printed and published by N. Harding, 7 Werburgh–Street, 1862) p. 19.

35 Desmond Bowen, *The Protestant Crusade* p. 104.

36 B. Scalé, *Map of Leitrim* (1776), Taylor and Skinner, *Maps of the Roads of Ireland* surveyed 1777 (London and Dublin, 1778) p. 234.

37 Henry Crookshank, *History of Methodism in Ireland* (3 vols, Belfast, 1885) ii, p. 261.

38 Samuel Lewis, *Topographical Dictionary of Ireland*, (London 1837) i, p. 517.

39 *Report of the trial ...* p. 13.

40 *Report of the trial ...* p. 10.

41 *Report of the trial ...* p. 11.

42 *Report of the trial ...* p. 33.

43 *Report of the trial ...* p. 5.

44 *Leitrim Journal*, 29 January 1855.

45 *Roscommon and Leitrim Gazette*, 5 May 1827.

46 National Archives, Dublin, State of the Country Papers, 2832/11 (hereinafter N.A., S.O.C. Papers)

47 N.A., S.O.C. Papers 2832/16.

48 N.A., S.O.C. Papers 2832/16.

49 *Roscommon and Leitrim Gazette*, 12 January 1828.

50 N.A., S.O.C. Papers 2832/19.

51 N.A., S.O.C. Papers 2832/19.

52 N.A., S.O.C. Papers 2832/11.

53 *Report from the select committee appointed to enquire into the nature, char-acter, extent and tendency of Orange lodges, associations or societies in Ireland, with the minutes of evidence and Appendix H.C.* 1835, [377] xv, Appendix to Report, p. 42.

54 *Report of the trial ...* p. 12.

55 *Report of the trial ...* p. 4.

56 Register of Members, Lodge 919 in Library, Grand Masonic Lodge, Molesworth St. Dublin.

57 Letter dated 23 October 1856, Folder I, Lodge 187 (Drumkeerin) in Library, Grand Masonic Lodge, Molesworth St, Dublin.

58 *Leitrim Journal*, 29 January 1852.

59 *Leitrim Journal*, 29 January 1852.

60 Register of Members, Masonic Lodge 919. Letter dated 23 December 1852, Folder I Masonic Lodge 919.

61 Letter dated 29 May 1826, Folder I Masonic Lodge 919.

62 *List of masonic lodges in Leitrim*, Library Grand Masonic Lodge, Molesworth St, Dublin.

63 Peter Clancy, *Historical notices of the parish of Inishmagrath*, (Privately published, 1958) pp 75–77

64 *Leitrim Journal*, 29 January 1852.

65 Rev Canon Swanzy, 'Lists of parochial clergy of the late established church in the diocese of Kilmore' in *Breifne Antiquarian Society Journal* ii, no. 3, (1927) p. 399.

66 N.A., S.O.C. Papers, 2832/16.

67 Lewis, *Topographical Dictionary*, i, p. 24.

68 *Report of the trial ...* p. 12.

69 N.A., S.O.C. Papers, 2832/16.

70 Lewis, *Topographical Dictionary*, i, p. 24.

71 *Report of the trial ...* p. 11.

72 Peter Clancy, *Historical Notices of the Parish of Inishmagrath*, p. 100 and p. 106.

73 Rev T. Cunningham, 'The 1766 Religious Census Kilmore and Ardagh' in *Breifne* i, no. 4, 1961 p. 358.

74 Peter Clancy, *Historical Notices of the Parish of Inishmagrath*, p. 106. Commission of Public Instruction Ireland, Province of Armagh, Diocese of Kilmore pp 34 A and 35A.

75 N.A., S.O.C. Papers, 2832/17.

THE TRIAL

1 Raymond McGovern, 'Father Tom Maguire, Polemicist, Popular Preacher and Patriot' in *Breifne* iv, no. 14, (1971) pp 277–288.

2 Francis J. McKiernan, *Diocese of Kilmore* (Cavan 1989) p. 180.

3 *Report of the trial in the case of Barw. M'Garahan versus the Rev T Maguire before Baron Smith and a special Jury*, (Dublin), printed and published by N Harding, 7 Werburgh–Street, 1862 p. 5.

4 *Report of the trial ... p. 17.*

5 Peter, Clancy *Historical Notices of the Parish of Inishmagrath*, (Privately published, 1958) p. 59–60.

6 Royal Irish Academy MS 23042, ff. 37–39.

7 Fagan, W., *The Life and Times of Daniel O'Connell*, (2 vols Cork, 1847–8), ii, p. 471.

8 *Roscommon and Leitrim Gazette*, 22 December 1827.

9 *Report of the trial ... p. 34.*

10 William Joseph O'Neill Daunt, *Eighty Five Years of Irish History 1800–1885* (2 vols. London, 1886), i, pp 129–130.

11 *Important Judgement given on Monday the 11th of February 1828 by the Hon. Sir William Cusack Smith, Bart. one of the Barons of His Majesty's Court of Exchequer in Ireland, on a motion to set aside the verdict obtained by the defendant in the case of McGarrahan v. The Rev T. Maguire. (Dublin) 1828.* (Richard Coyne, Capel St.) p. 8.

12 J. Roderick, O Flanagan, *The Bar Life of Daniel O'Connell*, (Dublin, 1875), pp 143–144.

13 Maurice R. O'Connell, (ed.), *The Correspondence of Daniel O'Connell 1824–28* (8 vols, Dublin 1970–84) iii, p. 62.

14 *Important Judgement given on Monday the 11th of February 1828 by the Hon. Sir William Cusack Smith ... p. 9.*

15 J. Roderick O Flanagan, *The bar life of Daniel O'Connell*, (Dublin, 1875) p. 138.

16 *Roscommon and Leitrim Gazette*, 1 December 1827.

17 Wilmot Harrison, *Memorable Dublin houses* 1971.

18 Charles Chenevix Trench, *The Great Dan* (London) 1986 pp 148–9.

19 T. W. Moody F. X. Martin; F.J. Byrne (eds.), *A New History of Ireland:* viii (Oxford, 1982) p. 314.

20 *Roscommon and Leitrim Gazette*, 15 December 1827.

21 *Report of the trial ... p. 33.*

22 O'Flanagan, *The bar life of Daniel O'Connell*, p. 145.

23 *Report of the trial ... p. 1.*

24 O'Flanagan, *The bar life of Daniel O'Connell*, pp 141–143.

25 *Report of the trial ... pp 1–6.*

26 *Roscommon and Leitrim Gazette*, 15 December 1827.

27 *Roscommon and Leitrim Gazette*, 22 December 1827.

28 O'Flanagan, *The bar life of Daniel O'Connell*, p. 143.

29 *Report of the trial ... pp 6–15.*

30 *Report of the trial ... pp 15–17.*

31 *Report of the trial ... pp 17–18.*

32 *Report of the trial ... p. 18.*

33 O'Connell, *The Correspondence of Daniel O'Connell* iii p. 365.

34 *Report of the trial ... pp 18–31.*

35 *Report of the trial ... pp 31–33.*

36 *Report of the trial ... p. 35.*

37 *Report of the trial ... pp 34–35.*

38 *Report of the trial ... p. 33–34.*

39 *Report of the trial ... p. 34.*

40 *Report of the trial ... p. 35.*

41 *Report of the trial ... p. 35.*

42 *Report of the trial ... pp 35–42.*

43 *Roscommon and Leitrim Gazette*, 22 December 1827.
44 *Report of the trial* ... pp 42–50.
45 *Report of the trial* ... p. 50.

THE FALL OUT

1 Maurice R. O'Connell, *The Correspondence of Daniel O'Connell* 1824–28 iii p. 365.
2 *Sligo Journal* 8 January 1828, *The Enniskillen Chronicle and Erne Packet*, 20 December 1827.
3 *Roscommon and Leitrim Gazette*, 22 December 1827.
4 *Roscommon and Leitrim Gazette*, 22 December 1827.
5 *Roscommon and Leitrim Gazette*, 22 December 1827.
6 *Roscommon and Leitrim Gazette*, 22 December 1827.
7 *Sligo Journal*, 1 January 1828.
8 *The Nymphs of Drumkeerin; or, Love and Scalteen!! An Humorous Poem by II. I. Comus* (Dublin) 1827, Pub. Thomas Haydock and Son, Printers No. 8, Lower Exchange-Street.
9 *The Enniskillen Chronicle and Erne Packet*, 24 January 1828.
10 *Roscommon and Leitrim Gazette*, 5 January 1828.
11 *Important Judgement given on Monday the 11th of February 1828 by the Hon. Sir William Cusack Smith* ... p. 34.
12 *Roscommon and Leitrim Gazette*, 5 January 1828.
13 *Roscommon and Leitrim Gazette*, 23 February 1828.
14 *Roscommon and Leitrim Gazette*, 23 February 1828, 1 March 1828.
15 N.A., S.O.C. Papers, 2832/17.
16 *Sligo Journal*, 8 January 1828.
17 *Sligo Journal*, 8 January 1828.
18 *Sligo Journal*, 8 January 1828.
19 *Sligo Journal*, 22 January 1828.
20 *Sligo Journal*, 2 February 1828, *Roscommon and Leitrim Gazette*, 12 January 1828.

21 *Decision of the Four Judges, in the case of McGarrahan versus Maguire on application being made for a New trial* (Dublin) 1828, Printed by Bentham and Hardy pp 12–14.
22 *Decision of the Four Judges ... New trial* (Dublin) 1828, Printed by Bentham and Hardy p. 14.
23 *Important Judgement given on Monday the 11th of February 1828 by the Hon. Sir William Cusack Smith* ... p. 36.
24 *Important Judgement given on Monday the 11th of February 1828 by the Hon. Sir William Cusack Smith* ... p. 5.
25 *Important Judgement given on Monday the 11th of February 1828 by the Hon. Sir William Cusack Smith* ... pp 7–8.
26 *Important Judgement given on Monday the 11th of February 1828 by the Hon. Sir William Cusack Smith* ... pp. 32–33.
27 *Important Judgement given on Monday the 11th of February 1828 by the Hon. Sir William Cusack Smith* ... pp 23–25.
28 *Important Judgement given on Monday the 11th of February 1828 by the Hon. Sir William Cusack Smith* ... p. 34.
29 *Important Judgement given on Monday the 11th of February 1828 by the Hon. Sir William Cusack Smith* ... p. 9.
30 *Important Judgement given on Monday the 11th of February 1828 by the Hon. Sir William Cusack Smith* ... p. 36.
31 *Roscommon and Leitrim Gazette*, 24 May 1828.

CONCLUSION

1 Ríonach Uí Ógáin, *Immortal Dan, Daniel O'Connell*, (Dublin, n.d.) p. 96, J N.Healy *Second book of Irish Ballads*, (Cork, 1979) p. 213.
2 Interview with Frank McGee aged 83 of Creevalea, Drumkeerin. 26 March 1986.
3 Uí Ógáin, *Immortal Dan, Daniel O'Connell*, p. 95.

4   Interview with Frank McGee aged 83 of Creevalea, Drumkeerin, 26 March 1986.

5   Dan Gallogly, *Sliabh an Iarainn Slopes* (1991) p. 173.

6   P. Ó Gallachair, *Where Erne and Drowes Meet the Sea* (n.p./1961) pp 60–61.

7   D. Gallogly, *Sliabh an Iarainn Slopes*, p. 173.

8   D. Gallogly, 'Kilmore Churches' in *Breifne* viii, no. 30, (1994) p. 433 and 443.

9   *False Weights and Measures of the protestant Curate of Cavan examined and exposed or the 'Inspector Inspected' in reply to the first great literary essay of the Rev James Collins A.M. entitled 'The Priests Detected'* by the Rev Thomas Maguire. Printed by Richard Coyne, 4 Capel St., Dublin 1833.

10 Healy, *Second book of Irish ballads* p. 213.

11 *Sligo Journal* 2 January 1828.

12 Rev Patrick Brady, 'Father Tom Maguire and the Clare Election' in *Breifne*, 1, No 1 (1959) pp 56–59.

13 Desmond Bowen, *The Protestant Crusade in Ireland 1800–1870* p. 107

14 D. Gallogly, *Sliabh an Iarainn Slopes*, p. 173.

15 Healy, *Second book of Irish ballads*, p. 213.

16 Interview with Frank McGee aged 83 of Creevalea, Drumkeerin, 26 March 1986.